A RANCHER'S HANDS

Victoria Vollmer

AuthorHouse™
1663 Liberty Drive
Bloomington, IN 47403
www.authorhouse.com
Phone: 833-262-8899

Because of the dynamic nature of the Internet, any web addresses or links contained in this book may have changed since publication and may no longer be valid. The views expressed in this work are solely those of the author and do not necessarily reflect the views of the publisher, and the publisher hereby disclaims any responsibility for them.

Any people depicted in stock imagery provided by Getty Images are models, and such images are being used for illustrative purposes only.
Certain stock imagery © Getty Images.

This book is printed on acid-free paper.

ISBN: 978-1-6655-5120-5 (sc)
978-1-6655-5122-9 (hc)
978-1-6655-5121-2 (e)

Print information available on the last page.

Published by AuthorHouse 02/18/2022

authorHOUSE®

About the Art

These hand drawn illustrations may not be masterpieces to some, but there is a reason behind that. The beauty in creating these pieces of art is because ranching isn't always beautiful. Ranching is something that has some downfalls that may be discouraging; however, the positives outweigh the negative. Many believe that ranchers are just in it for the money, which is not the case. Rancher's love what they do, even though it takes a tremendous amount of work to take care of the animals that they have. They do this by making sure they are as healthy as can be each day. There are no days off for ranchers because animals always need to be taken care of, just like you do! Ranching is something we take pride and joy in every single day. The next time you see a rancher, be sure to ask them what they do and why they do it, then you too will see the art in what goes into a ranch!

Thank you!

Special thank you to Prairie Topp, owner of Topp Herefords, McCumber Angus Genetics, and Circle V Angus Ranch for inspiring the watercolor art found throughout the book.

Dedicated to

all Rancher's

A rancher's hands do many things on a ranch...

A rancher's hands drive equipment to make food for their animals.

A rancher's hands help the vet do research to make sure the animals are feeling their best.

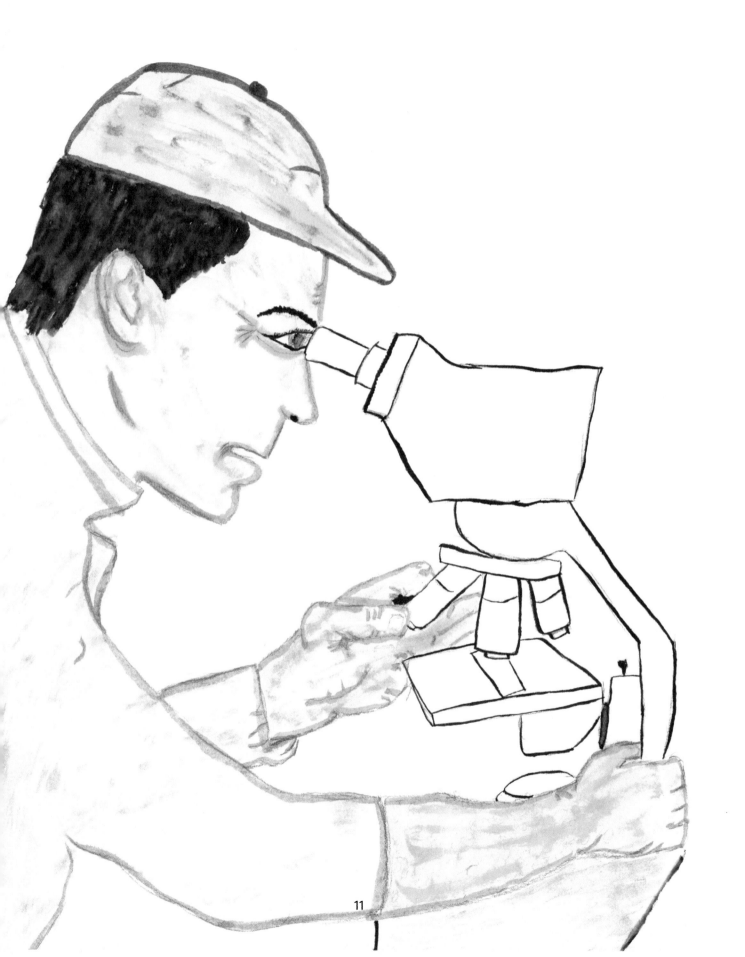

A rancher's hands keeps the area clean where animals live.

A rancher's hands bring animals home when the weather gets bad or sometimes when they need medicine because they are sick.

A rancher's hands patiently care for all their animals, big or little on the ranch.

A rancher's hands groom and clip
animals when they need it, just like
you do when you get a haircut!

A rancher's hands carefully pours

out medicine to give to animals, just

like a doctor takes care of you!

A rancher's hands are the most

important tool on the ranch.

They are used to keep their animals

safe, healthy, and happy!

Sponsors

Circle V Angus Ranch

McCumber Angus Ranch

Topp Herefords Ranch

Lampert Farms

Hat Creek Cattle Company "We don't rent pigs"

Briss Oil Company

T-T Ranch

Grandma Vollmer

Holecek Ranch

Anonymous Sponsors

Printed in the United States
by Baker & Taylor Publisher Services